Instant Fancybox

Enhance the look of your web pages using the lightweight
and highly customizable jQuery plugin Fancybox

Kyle Diedrick

PUBLISHING
BIRMINGHAM - MUMBAI

Instant Fancybox

First published: October 2013

Production Reference: 1241013

Published by Packt Publishing Ltd.
Livery Place
35 Livery Street
Birmingham B3 2PB, UK.

ISBN 978-1-78328-207-4

www.packtpub.com

Credits

Author
Kyle Diedrick

Reviewers
Noah W. E. Gilmore

Kurn J. La Montagne

Acquisition Editors
Usha Iyer

James Jones

Commissioning Editor
Mohammed Fahad

Technical Editors
Siddhi Rane

Tarunveer Shetty

Copy Editors
Alisha Aranha

Adithi Shetty

Project Coordinator
Amey Sawant

Proofreader
Bernadette Watkins

Production Coordinator
Kyle Albuquerque

Cover Work
Kyle Albuquerque

Cover Image
Abhinash Sahu

About the Author

Kyle Diedrick is a software engineer living in Irvine, California. He has been working on websites for the past 10 years. He has also been blogging about software development for roughly four years on his website, Graphics Unplugged. He has substantial experience working on websites using JavaScript, CSS, HTML, PHP, and most recently, CoffeeScript. He first discovered the Fancybox jQuery plugin while working at Great Wolf Resorts in 2010. He began using the plugin because of its flexibility.

Kyle does freelance website design and development through his personal website, Graphics Unplugged. Graphics Unplugged focuses primarily on websites but has recently begun expanding into mobile application development for both iOS and Android. He also writes blogs about website design and development.

I would like to thank all the people that have helped me learn and evolve as a developer and everyone who has been there for me to bounce ideas off of or guided me when I wasn't sure about the path to take. I'd like to thank the Madison Area Technical College for having a fantastic software development program and my instructors who were passionate about the field. It was great to have so many helpful people in one place.

I would also like to thank my parents for all of their support while I found my way through school and into the great field I work in now.

About the Reviewers

Noah W. E. Gilmore is a web developer and software engineer living in the San Francisco Bay area. He has experience building dynamic and intuitive user interfaces and large-scale web applications. He is a web enthusiast and enjoys creating new and innovative solutions to critical problems.

He created his first website at the age of 10, and since then he has done freelance web designing and development around the Bay Area, in addition to working for an American Internet company, Yelp.

He is a student at the University of California, Berkeley, where he is a member of various software engineering groups including Cal Blueprint (`calblueprint.org`), which provides free software solutions to non-profit organizations. He believes strongly in harnessing his skills as an engineer to create technology that works toward the betterment of society at large.

I would like to thank my mother, my father, and my younger brother for encouraging me to do what I love, and for teaching me that exploration and curiosity are important skills. I would also like to thank my entire family and my friends in Chicago and at Berkeley for their help and support in getting me where I am today—I would be lying if I said that I did this myself.

Kurn J. La Montagne is a software developer (with a strong preference for web), open source hacker, freelance developer, CakePHP Baker, and nature lover living in the tropical Caribbean island of Saint Lucia. He is employed as a Web Application Developer with the National Insurance Corporation where he enjoys working on a variety of web-based projects.

Prior to working for the National Insurance Corporation, he studied computing at the University of the Southern Caribbean, Trinidad, and was part of the team which won the first annual Teleios Code Jam programming competition, an initiative of Teleios Systems Limited, which encourages students to use information technology to solve problems and facilitate development in the Caribbean region.

He spends most of his free time hacking on open source projects and is the creator of the CakePHP Highcharts plugin (available on GitHub). He enjoys working with many established frameworks, as well as trying out new ones. He is currently working with CakePHP, Lithium, and Wordpress for various small projects. He is looking forward to learning about non-SQL databases and Node.js. For the past three years, he has lectured part time at the St Lucia extension campus of the University of the Southern Caribbean.

I'd like to thank my wonderful soul mate Fayola for putting up with all the busy hours and my incessant talking about things she doesn't really understand. I'd also like to thank the fantastic people at Packt Publishing for giving me the opportunity to contribute to this book.

www.PacktPub.com

Support files, eBooks, discount offers and more

You might want to visit www.PacktPub.com for support files and downloads related to your book.

Did you know that Packt offers eBook versions of every book published, with PDF and ePub files available? You can upgrade to the eBook version at www.PacktPub.com and as a print book customer, you are entitled to a discount on the eBook copy. Get in touch with us at service@packtpub.com for more details.

At www.PacktPub.com, you can also read a collection of free technical articles, sign up for a range of free newsletters and receive exclusive discounts and offers on Packt books and eBooks.

http://PacktLib.PacktPub.com

Do you need instant solutions to your IT questions? PacktLib is Packt's online digital book library. Here, you can access, read and search across Packt's entire library of books.

Why Subscribe?

- ▶ Fully searchable across every book published by Packt
- ▶ Copy and paste, print, and bookmark content
- ▶ On demand and accessible via web browser

Free Access for Packt account holders

If you have an account with Packt at www.PacktPub.com, you can use this to access PacktLib today and view nine entirely free books. Simply use your login credentials for immediate access.

Table of Contents

Preface

Instant Fancybox is a jQuery lightbox plugin, which is very versatile and customizable. A lightbox is essentially an in-page pop-up window. These have become the de facto way to show pop-up content on the web for various reasons, including interaction between lightboxes and the main content via JavaScript. Actual pop-up windows are frequently blocked by browsers because people find actual pop-up windows (if they are not blocked) to be annoying. Fancybox has several very cool features that make it a powerful lightbox tool such as built-in image galleries and slide shows. It is responsive (that is, it adjusts to the size of the browser window), it can load many different types of content, and it has a very powerful API and settings system that allow it to be easily extended and customized.

This book covers Version 2 of the plugin. It will cover all of the functionality that Fancybox provides, as well as a step-by-step walkthrough of some of the ways to use Fancybox. The book starts with installing the plugin and works its way from loading a simple image all the way to adding custom functionality around the Fancybox pop up.

What this book covers

Installing Fancybox (Simple), will show how to download and install the code for the Fancybox plugin in an HTML file.

Fancybox with a single image (Simple), will start out with a simple first crack at Fancybox. The simplest way to begin learning Fancybox is to create a basic HTML page, which shows a single image in Fancybox.

Creating an image gallery (Simple), will show how to create an image gallery that can be expanded inside Fancybox. The image gallery can then be viewed as an image slideshow.

Displaying YouTube videos (Intermediate), will show how to display a YouTube video inside Fancybox. We also cover getting the necessary information about the video from the YouTube website.

Loading content via AJAX (Intermediate), will show how to display an HTML file from a web server using Fancybox's AJAX content type. We'll also cover changing the error message that Fancybox displays if it cannot load the content.

Loading additional types of content (Intermediate), will show how Fancybox can load other types of content beyond just images, videos, and asynchronous HTML. We will also look at using Fancybox to load any iframe content, Flash (SWF) files, and inline HTML.

Adding thumbnails to a gallery (Simple), will show how Fancybox can display thumbnails of the images in our gallery. We will also look at changing the position of the thumbnails and changing where the thumbnail images are loaded from.

Adding buttons to image slideshows (Simple), will show how Fancybox can display buttons to interact with image slide shows. We'll take a look at using Fancybox to display these buttons and at ways we can customize them.

Customizing other helpers (Intermediate), will introduce helpers, which are additional features that are optional but technically a part of Fancybox. Here we take a look at two more helpers: image title and the transparent overlay.

Modifying styles and layout (Intermediate), will cover the ways Fancybox allows us to change the look and positioning of the Fancybox pop up.

Changing slideshow settings (Advanced), will look at changing all of the slide show related settings in Fancybox. This includes play speed, looping, automatically playing, and preloading images.

Adding custom styles (Intermediate), will show how Fancybox provides the ability to add custom classes to the Fancybox HTML. Here we take a look at how to add custom classes as well as the classes Fancybox uses by default.

Changing animation effects (Intermediate), will show how Fancybox allows us to change all of the animation effects. We take a look at changing all of the effects for opening and closing Fancybox as well as changing the effects for moving around inside an image slide show.

Changing keyboard shortcuts (Advanced), will show how Fancybox provides a handful of useful keyboard shortcuts by default. We will investigate changing these defaults as well as adding our own keyboard shortcuts while keeping the defaults.

Interacting with Fancybox (Advanced), will show how Fancybox provides a number of ways to open, close, or otherwise interact with the Fancybox pop up programmatically. We take a look at using JavaScript code to open and close the Fancybox pop up.

Manipulating image slideshows (Advanced), will show how Fancybox also provides API functions to interact with image slideshows. In this section we create some custom links, which trigger the standard next, previous, and play/pause functionality.

Listening for Fancybox events (Advanced), will show how to use the Fancybox callback events to run code at key points of the Fancybox pop up's life, including the following: just after it is displayed, just before it is closed, and just as the slideshow is paused. We also list all of the callback events that Fancybox provides.

What you need for this book

For this book you will need at least a web browser and a text editor. For the recipe on AJAX content you will also need a web server which can host an HTML file. You will also need an Internet connection to download the Fancybox plugin and jQuery JavaScript and CSS files.

Who this book is for

This book is aimed at frontend web developers looking to learn about the jQuery plugin Fancybox. It is expected that the reader should have some knowledge of JavaScript syntax as well as jQuery. It is also expected that the reader should have a basic understanding of HTML and CSS. However, I believe anyone with even a little experience in JavaScript, HTML, and CSS can pick up this book and learn how to use the Fancybox plugin.

Conventions

In this book, you will find a number of text styles that distinguish between different kinds of information. Here are some examples of these styles and an explanation of their meaning.

Code words in text, database table names, folder names, filenames, file extensions, pathnames, dummy URLs, and user input are shown as follows: "Create a folder called `images` alongside the `index.html` file and put the image in the folder."

A block of code is set as follows:

```
<!DOCTYPE html>
<html>
<head>
    <title>Chapter 1</title>
</head>
<body>
    <h1>Installing Fancybox</h1>
</body>
</html>
```

New terms and **important words** are shown in bold. Words that you see on the screen, in menus or dialog boxes for example, appear in the text like this: "click on the **share** tab as shown in the following screenshot:"

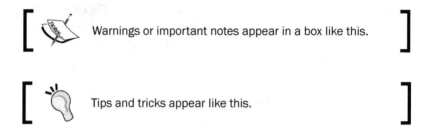

Warnings or important notes appear in a box like this.

Tips and tricks appear like this.

Reader feedback

Feedback from our readers is always welcome. Let us know what you think about this book—what you liked or may have disliked. Reader feedback is important for us to develop titles that you really get the most out of.

To send us general feedback, simply send an e-mail to feedback@packtpub.com, and mention the book title via the subject of your message.

If there is a book that you need and would like to see us publish, please send us a note in the **SUGGEST A TITLE** form on www.packtpub.com or e-mail suggest@packtpub.com.

If there is a topic that you have expertise in and you are interested in either writing or contributing to a book, see our author guide on www.packtpub.com/authors.

Customer support

Now that you are the proud owner of a Packt book, we have a number of things to help you to get the most from your purchase.

Downloading the example code

You can download the example code files for all Packt books you have purchased from your account at http://www.PacktPub.com. If you purchased this book elsewhere, you can visit http://www.PacktPub.com/support and register to have the files e-mailed directly to you.

Errata

Although we have taken every care to ensure the accuracy of our content, mistakes do happen. If you find a mistake in one of our books—maybe a mistake in the text or the code—we would be grateful if you would report this to us. By doing so, you can save other readers from frustration and help us improve subsequent versions of this book. If you find any errata, please report them by visiting `http://www.packtpub.com/support`, selecting your book, clicking on the **errata submission form** link, and entering the details of your errata. Once your errata are verified, your submission will be accepted and the errata will be uploaded on our website, or added to any list of existing errata, under the Errata section of that title. Any existing errata can be viewed by selecting your title from `http://www.packtpub.com/support`.

Piracy

Piracy of copyright material on the Internet is an ongoing problem across all media. At Packt, we take the protection of our copyright and licenses very seriously. If you come across any illegal copies of our works, in any form, on the Internet, please provide us with the location address or website name immediately so that we can pursue a remedy.

Please contact us at `copyright@packtpub.com` with a link to the suspected pirated material.

We appreciate your help in protecting our authors, and our ability to bring you valuable content.

Questions

You can contact us at `questions@packtpub.com` if you are having a problem with any aspect of the book, and we will do our best to address it.

Instant Fancybox

Welcome to *Instant Fancybox*. The goal of this book is to teach you how to install, use, and customize the Fancybox plugin for jQuery. This book discusses in detail the second version of the Fancybox plugin. The first version will not be covered because Fancybox2 is much more rich in features and is more powerful than its predecessor, and I strongly suggest using it or switching to it! This book assumes that the reader has some basic understanding of web development including knowledge of HTML, CSS, and very basic JavaScript.

Installing Fancybox (Simple)

We're going to start by creating a basic HTML page, which will have jQuery and the Fancybox plugin loaded on it. We'll walk through the steps to get the plugin and make sure that it is loading on the page.

Getting ready

To install the Fancybox plugin, you will need only two things: a text editor or some way to create HTML, CSS, and JavaScript files, and an Internet connection to obtain the plugin.

How to do it...

1. Go to the Fancyapps website, `http://fancyapps.com/fancybox/`.
2. Scroll down to the download link and download the files.
3. Create a folder that will be the location of our demo HTML page.
4. Extract the zip file that was just downloaded and move the folder to the directory that will be used for the page. Rename the folder to `fancybox`.

5. Create a basic HTML page inside the folder. Here's a sample of a really basic HTML5 page with a title:

```
<!DOCTYPE html>
<html>
<head>
    <title>Chapter 1</title>
</head>
<body>
    <h1>Installing Fancybox</h1>
</body>
</html>
```

Downloading the example code

You can download the example code files for all Packt books you have purchased from your account at http://www.PacktPub.com. If you purchased this book elsewhere, you can visit http://www.PacktPub.com/support and register to have the files e-mailed directly to you.

6. Add the following script tags to load jQuery and Fancybox just under the `<title>` tag:

```
<link rel="stylesheet"
  href="fancybox/source/jquery.fancybox.css?v=2.1.4"
  type="text/css" media="screen" />
<script type="text/javascript"
  src="https://ajax.googleapis.com/ajax/libs/jquery/2.0.0/
    jquery.min.js"></script>
<script type="text/javascript"
  src="fancybox/source/jquery.fancybox.pack.js?v=2.1.4">
</script>
```

First, we load CSS for Fancybox, then jQuery (via Google CDN), and then the main Fancybox JavaScript file.

7. Now that we have everything loaded on the page, let's load the page and check for any JavaScript errors. If everything has worked, there should be no errors on the page and you should be able to open the console and type `$.fancybox`. You will see something like the following code if everything has worked:

```
function (){b.open.apply(this,arguments)}
```

If you see that undefined Fancybox is not loaded on the page, check the file paths that you have in the `src` attribute of your script tags. Remember that we changed the directory to be called `fancybox` in step four.

How it works...

We now have a basic HTML page, which has jQuery and the Fancybox plugin loaded. The download from the Fancybox website includes the full source of the plugin in a non-minified form, the minified version (which we are currently loading on the page), the necessary images and CSS files, and a folder that includes some demos.

We are loading jQuery from the Google CDN for several major reasons:

▸ By using the Google CDN, we don't have to pay to host the file when we are using Fancybox on a live website.

▸ Since it is common for other websites to use the Google CDN for jQuery, it is likely that users coming to our website will have the file cached. This makes our website load faster!

▸ Using jQuery from the Google CDN also allows us to easily update the version of jQuery that is being used.

 In the previous example code, we are using jQuery version 2.0, which does not support IE 6, 7, and 8. If you need to support any of these browsers, use an older version of jQuery such as 1.9.2. Fancybox works with both versions.

Because we are using jQuery from the Google CDN, it will only work when the computer has access to the Internet. If you want to do any work while not having access to the Internet, you will need to download a copy of jQuery onto your computer.

If you looked around on the Fancybox website, you may have noticed that all of the files that are considered part of Fancybox are not included. For the very basic use of Fancybox, these other files are not necessary. These other files add extra functionalities to Fancybox, but Fancybox works just fine without them. Later in this book, we will discuss what extra functionalities these files provide.

Fancybox with a single image (Simple)

Now that we have the Fancybox plugin loaded on the page, let's make it actually do something. To start things off, we'll simply have Fancybox load a single image.

Getting ready

Before we get started, we need to set up a few more files. First, find an image to use. It should be a decently large image so we can see Fancybox do its thing. Create a folder called `images` alongside the `index.html` file and put the image in the folder. Now that we have an image to use, let's make Fancybox use it. We're going to build on top of the code used previously, when we learned how to install Fancybox.

How to do it...

1. Create a new JavaScript file called `scripts.js` in the same directory as our `index.html` file.

2. Inside the `scripts.js` file, we need to add some code to the jQuery `document.ready` function. To get things started, let's just add a `console.log()` function call, so that we can see the function is being called:

    ```
    $(function() {
      console.log("hello world");
    });
    ```

    By passing an anonymous function to jQuery (`$`), we are telling jQuery that we want all of the code inside the anonymous function to be run when the document is finished loading.

3. Now that we have our `scripts.js` file created, we need to add it to the HTML file. Inside the `index.html` file, under the last script tag that we previously added, we need to add the following:

    ```
    <script type="text/javascript" src="scripts.js">
    </script>
    ```

4. Now that we have a call to the `console.log` function, you should see `hello world` in the console in your browser when you reload the file. You should be able to find the console in the developer tools for the web browser of your choice. In Firefox, the **Web Developer** menu is available under the main menu (by clicking on the Firefox button at the top-left corner). In Chrome, it is under the main menu; go to **Tools | JavaScript console**. In Internet Explorer, it is located in the menu under the **F12 developer tools** tab.

 Having access to the JavaScript console is important for many of the guides in this book. If your browser of choice does not have a JavaScript console, it is highly recommended that you download a browser that does.

5. Before we get the JavaScript written to load the image, let's create the HTML tag for the link that will be clicked to load it. Just under the `<h1>` tag add the following:

```
<a id="show-fancybox" href="images/waterfall.png">Show Fancybox</a>
```

You will want to replace the `href` attribute of the anchor tag to be your image's location. In the example, I have an image called `waterfall.png` in the `images` folder. If you refresh the page and click on the link, the image should be displayed in the browser.

6. Now let's move back to the `scripts.js` file. We know that our function is being loaded, so we can remove the call to the `console.log function`.

7. Next, let's call Fancybox on our anchor tag with the following code:

```
$(function() {
  $('#show-fancybox').fancybox();
});
```

You should see your image displayed in a Fancybox pop up as shown in the following screenshot:

How it works...

Let's take a deeper look at what is going on in step two. Behind the scenes, jQuery is listening for several browser events, which the different browsers fire when the document has finished loading. Then, it will run the function that is provided. You may also see this in a slightly longer format, but it is doing the same thing:

```
$(document).ready(function() {…});
```

Let's talk a little bit more about the last step. In the given code, $('#show-fancybox') retrieves a jQuery object, which represents our anchor tag. fancybox() is the call to Fancybox, which makes it work. Fancybox then takes the href attribute of the link and attempts to retrieve the URL provided. In our case, the URL points to the image we wanted Fancybox to display.

The directory structure used in this recipe will be used throughout the book. Our scripts file will always be `scripts.js`, all of our images will always be in the `images` directory, and we'll always have the `index.html` file.

There's more...

So what else can we do with the single image functionality of Fancybox? Let's take a look at some additional touches to our single image.

Adding a caption

What if we wanted to add a caption to the image? Fortunately, it's incredibly simple. To add a caption to the image, all we have to do is add the title attribute to the link, shown as follows:

```
<a id="show-fancybox" href="images/waterfall.png"
   title="Just a little waterfall">Show Fancybox</a>
```

Now when Fancybox opens up the title `Just a little waterfall`, it will show up under our image.

Using a thumbnail

Using a thumbnail on the page, for the user to click on, is also very easy. All we have to do is add the thumbnail as an `<img />` tag, shown as follows:

```
<a id="show-fancybox" href="images/waterfall.png"
   title="Just a little waterfall">
   <img src="images/waterfall-small.png"></a>
```

In the example, the `waterfall-small.png` file is the thumbnail. Now the thumbnail is displayed on the page, and clicking on it displays the larger image in the Fancybox pop up.

Creating an image gallery (Simple)

Fancybox also provides some great image gallery and slideshow functionality. Let's take a look at what is involved in creating a Fancybox gallery.

Getting ready

Before we get started, we need to find a handful of images that we can use for the gallery. Find four to five images to use for the gallery and put them in the `images` folder.

How to do it...

1. Add the following links to the images to the `index.html` file:

```
<a class="fancybox"
  href="images/waterfall.png">Waterfall</a>
<a class="fancybox" href="images/frozen-
  lake.png">Frozen Lake</a>
<a class="fancybox" href="images/road-in-
  forest.png">Road in Forest</a>
<a class="fancybox" href="images/boston.png">Boston</a>
```

 The anchor tags no longer have an ID, but a class. It is important that they all have the same class so that Fancybox knows about them.

2. Change our call to the Fancybox plugin in the `scripts.js` file to use the class that all of the links have instead of `show-fancybox ID`.

```
$(function() {
    // Using fancybox class instead of the show-fancybox ID
    $('.fancybox').fancybox();
});
```

3. Fancybox will now work on all of the images but they will not be part of the same gallery. To make images part of a gallery, we use the `rel` attribute of the anchor tags. Add `rel="gallery"` to all of the anchor tags, shown as follows:

```
<a class="fancybox" rel="gallery"
  href="images/waterfall.png">Waterfall</a>
<a class="fancybox" rel="gallery" href="images/frozen-
  lake.png">Frozen Lake</a>
<a class="fancybox" rel="gallery" href="images/road-
  in-forest.png">Road in Forest</a>
<a class="fancybox" rel="gallery"
  href="images/boston.png">Boston</a>
```

4. Now that we have added `rel="gallery"` to each of our anchor tags, you should see left and right arrows when you hover over the left-hand side or right-hand side of Fancybox. These arrows allow you to navigate between images as shown in the following screenshot:

How it works...

Fancybox determines that an image is part of a gallery using the `rel` attribute of the anchor tags. The order of the images is based on the order of the anchor tags on the page. This is important so that the slideshow order is exactly the same as a gallery of thumbnails without any additional work on our end.

We changed the ID of our single image to a class for the gallery because we wanted to call Fancybox on all of the links instead of just one. If we wanted to add more image links to the page, it would just be a matter of adding more anchor tags with the proper `href` values and the same class.

There's more...

So, what else can we do with the gallery functionality of Fancybox? Let's take a look at some of the other things that we could do with the gallery that we have currently.

Captions and thumbnails

All of the functionalities that we discussed for single images apply to galleries as well. So, if we wanted to add a thumbnail, it would just be a matter of adding an `img` tag inside the anchor tag instead of the text. If we wanted to add a caption, we can do so by adding the `title` attribute to our anchor tags.

Showing slideshow from one link

Let's say that we wanted to have just one link to open our gallery slideshow. This can be easily achieved by hiding the other links via CSS with the help of the following step:

1. We start by adding this `style` tag to the `<head>` tag just under the `<script>` tag for our `scripts.js` file, shown as follows:

```
<style type="text/css">
  .hidden {
    display: none;
  }
</style>
```

2. Now, we update the HTML file so that all but one of our anchor tags have the `hidden` class. Next, when we reload the page, we will see only one link. When you click on the link, you should still be able to navigate through the gallery just like all of the links were on the page.

```
<a class="fancybox" rel="gallery"
  href="images/waterfall.png">Image Gallery</a>
<div class="hidden">
  <a class="fancybox" rel="gallery"
    href="images/frozen-lake.png">Frozen Lake</a>
  <a class="fancybox" rel="gallery" href="images/road-
    in-forest.png">Road in Forest</a>
  <a class="fancybox" rel="gallery"
    href="images/boston.png">Boston</a>
</div>
```

Displaying YouTube videos (Intermediate)

Now that we've covered the basic image functionality for Fancybox, let's load a video from YouTube. Fancybox makes it easy to load any YouTube video in a pop-up window.

Getting ready

To start things off, we need to find a video we want to display. Go to YouTube and pick any video you like. We need to find the embed URL that YouTube provides.

On the YouTube page, for the video you want to use, click on the **Share** tab as shown in the following screenshot:

Next, click on the **Embed** link. A box will show up with some HTML code for an `iframe` tag as shown in the following screenshot:

Lastly, copy `src` of `iframe`. This is the embed link that we will use to show our video. Note that the protocol (`http` or `https`) may be left out of the iframe source. If no protocol is present inside the `src` attribute of the `iframe` tag, you will need to add it. Now that we have the source of our video, we can load it in Fancybox. Because we are using YouTube for our video, the entire YouTube API can be used in our embed URL. For the embed API see `https://developers.google.com/youtube/player_parameters`.

How to do it...

1. Create an anchor tag with a class of `show-popup`:

    ```
    <a class="show-popup">Wringing out Water on the ISS</a>
    ```

2. Add the `href` attribute and put the embed URL from the video that you selected as the value:

    ```
    <a class="show-popup"
      href="http://www.youtube.com/embed/o8TssbmY-GM">
      Wringing out Water on the ISS</a>
    ```

3. Add the `fancybox.iframe` class to the anchor tag:

    ```
    <a class="show-popup fancybox.iframe"
      href="http://www.youtube.com/embed/o8TssbmY-GM">
      Wringing out Water on the ISS</a>
    ```

4. Change the `scripts.js` file so that Fancybox is called on the `show-popup` class instead of the `fancybox` class:

    ```
    $('.show-popup').fancybox();
    ```

5. You should see your video loaded in Fancybox as shown in the following screenshot:

How it works...

There are two key advantages of using Fancybox to display YouTube videos. First, Fancybox is doing all of the additional work to load the embedded iframe on the page for us. Second, Fancybox needs to be told that it is loading content into an `iframe`. This is what the `fancybox.iframe` class does.

 YouTube allows us to load videos via secure (`https`) or nonsecure (`http`) connections. If you need to load the video on a secure page, make sure the `href` attribute is using `https`.

Once Fancybox is told that it needs to load the content as the iframe type, it will construct an iframe to load the URL provided in the `href` attribute. Fancybox also adds a handful of necessary attributes to the constructed iframe. The necessary attributes are `ID`, `name`, and `class`, which allow Fancybox to identify the iframe.

Other attributes of particular interest are `frameborder="0"` and `allowfullscreen`. The `frameborder` attribute tells iframe not to have any border. The `allowfullscreen` attribute (as well as the `webkitallowfullscreen` and `mozallowfullscreen` attributes) allows a method to be called from JavaScript to expand the iframe to 100 percent of the screen. This functionality is only supported in modern browsers. If you are interested in learning more about putting iframes into fullscreen mode, visit the Mozilla Developer Network page on the subject: `https://developer.mozilla.org/en-US/docs/DOM/Using_fullscreen_mode`. There are also two attributes that are no longer used in many browsers, `vspace` and `hspace`, but are used to support older browsers.

There's more...

Because we are working with external content, there is not a lot more that we can do in addition to the standard functionality of Fancybox. However, there are some other ways to tell Fancybox what to do with the content that we want to load. We can also leverage the YouTube API to provide a thumbnail for our video.

Other ways to set the content type

There are other ways to tell Fancybox that we are going to load the iframe content as well. One of the other options is to add another attribute to the anchor tag, `data-fancybox-type`. For our link, we will use the following code:

```
<a class="show-popup" data-fancybox-type="iframe" href="http://www.
youtube.com/embed/o8TssbmY-GM">Wringing out Water on the ISS</a>
```

The third option is to set the content type via a setting. Settings are passed to Fancybox via a JavaScript object. For our link, we would need to remove the `data-fancybox-type` attribute from the anchor tag so it looks like the following code:

```
<a class="show-popup" href="http://www.youtube.com/embed/o8TssbmY-
GM">Wringing out Water on the ISS</a>
```

We would also need to modify our `scripts.js` file, so that we pass the `type` setting to Fancybox as follows:

```
$(".show-popup").fancybox({type: "iframe"});
```

In the given code, we have set the `type` setting to be `"iframe"`. The `type` setting will override any other way we have set the content type to be loaded, so it should only be used when absolutely necessary. The best solution is to use the `data-fancybox-type` attribute, since it allows us to be fairly semantic (our HTML describes what it is going to do) and doesn't cause trouble with other calls to Fancybox.

For example, if we wanted to keep our image gallery on the page, we can keep our call to Fancybox the same for both the gallery and the video, as long as we set the `type` setting using the `data-fancybox-type` attribute or the class. If we used the setting, all of the images would be loaded as iframes, which stops Fancybox from shrinking our images to fit inside the pop up. It also stops us from accessing any of the content inside the Fancybox pop up using JavaScript because browsers treat iframes as separate pages from the main document.

Adding a thumbnail for the video

Adding a thumbnail for the video is very easy. We'll use the YouTube API to get a video thumbnail and add it to the page. YouTube provides access to four thumbnail images for any video. To make things simple, we'll just use the default image. The basic thumbnail URL looks like `http://img.youtube.com/vi/<video-id>/default.jpg`.

This URL is the default structure for any thumbnail from YouTube. We can replace `default.jpg` with `0.jpg`, `1.jpg`, `2.jpg`, `3.jpg`, `hqdefault.jpg`, `mqdefault.jpg`, or `maxresdefault.jpg` to load different thumbnails. For the video used in the demo, the video ID is `o8TssbmY-GM`, so the URL for the default thumbnail will be `http://img.youtube.com/vi/o8TssbmY-GM/default.jpg`. Now, we can just add this as an `img` tag inside our link to the video as follows:

```
<a class="show-popup" data-fancybox-type="iframe" href="http://www.
youtube.com/embed/o8TssbmY-GM"><img src="http://img.youtube.com/vi/
o8TssbmY-GM/default.jpg"></a>
```

We now have a thumbnail for our video that can be clicked on and the video loads in Fancybox.

Loading content via AJAX (Intermediate)

A common way to load additional HTML content is through asynchronous connections, commonly called **AJAX** (**Asynchronous JavaScript and XML**), but it is common to use AJAX to refer to all asynchronous JavaScript. Let's take a look at having Fancybox load content from our server asynchronously.

Getting ready

Up until this point all of the examples can work without a web server. If you have not been running examples on a web server, you will need to use one for this example. It does not matter which one you use, though I would recommend using a package that includes Apache such as **WAMP** if you are on Windows, MAMP if you are on Mac OS X, or XAMPP for Linux. A web server is required because JavaScript has a security feature that prevents communication with any server besides the one the original file was served from. If we do not use a server, it cannot determine the origin of any connections it attempts to make. If it cannot match the origin of the original connection, it cannot ensure that connections are being made to the same server, so it will prevent any connections from being made. For more information regarding the same-origin policy, see the Mozilla Developer Network: `https://developer.mozilla.org/en-US/docs/Web/JavaScript/Same_origin_policy_for_JavaScript`.

How to do it...

1. The first thing we need to do is to create a file to load asynchronously. Let's call the `async.html` file. This file should be created at the same directory level as the `index.html` file.

2. Next, we'll add some content to the file, so we can see that it is being loaded by Fancybox as follows:

    ```
    <style type="text/css">
    .special {
      color: lightblue;
      background: black;
      padding: 5px;
    }
    </style>
    <div class="special">This content has been loaded
    asynchronously!</div>
    ```

    Here, we have a `style` block with some inline styles to make the content stand out more, and a `div` tag with some text in it.

3. Now we need to create our link on the `index.html` page as follows:

```
<a class="show-popup" data-fancybox-type="ajax" href="async.
html">Load Asynchronously</a>
```

The link has a `show-popup` class and uses the `data-fancybox-type` attribute to tell Fancybox what type of data is being loaded.

4. Clicking on the link will make the HTML from `async.html` be displayed in Fancybox. You may briefly see the loading animation while the file is being loaded from your server, but since this is such a small amount of data, the loader will only display for a brief duration.

How it works...

Fancybox is actually doing quite a bit of work for us behind the scenes here. It relies on the jQuery `ajax` function to make the actual asynchronous request. Fancybox also provides us with a loading animation, which it displays and hides at the appropriate times, and provides a generic error message that will be displayed if the content we attempt to load doesn't exist. Fancybox then takes the `ajax` response (in this case, our HTML) and appends it into the Fancybox pop up.

The example we loaded just contains some simple HTML content and CSS. However, you can make a request to any kind of file. This means that you can request any file just like you would load it in the browser by entering the URL in the URL bar.

There's more...

Fancybox provides us with a lot of flexibility with its AJAX functionality. We can make a handful of customizations to the jQuery XHR object and change the HTML that is used for the error message.

Changing the error message

The generic error message used by Fancybox doesn't do much to tell the user what happened. Let's change the error message to make it easier for the user to know what they should do or try in case of an error. The error message that Fancybox provides is as follows:

```
The requested content cannot be loaded. Please try again later.
```

We can change the error message by leveraging the `tpl` (short for template) setting. In the `tpl` object, we can provide an error message to use, which can be any HTML. Let's change the error message to something different. In the `scripts.js` file, change the call to Fancybox to include the `error` template:

```
$('.show-popup').fancybox({
  tpl: {
    error: "<p>This is a different error message</p>"
  }
});
```

In the given code, we are passing an object to Fancybox with a `tpl` property. The `tpl` property is also an object and has a single property of `error`. The `error` property has our new error message. To see the error message load in Fancybox, simply change the `href` attribute of the link in the `index.html` file to point to a file that doesn't exist, shown as follows:

```
<a class="show-popup" data-fancybox-type="ajax" href="async-
  missing.html">Load Asynchronously</a>
```

Because the `async-missing.html` file doesn't exist on the web server, Fancybox will display our new error message.

Changing the jQuery XHR object

Fancybox allows us to provide additional settings to the jQuery AJAX request. Fancybox provides some default settings for AJAX requests, but we can override them. The `ajax` property of the settings object can contain any of the settings exposed in the jQuery `ajax` function, except for the few settings that Fancybox overrides. Fancybox overrides these `ajax` settings: `error`, `url`, and `success`.

The jQuery API provides exhaustive details on the functionality of the jQuery AJAX functionality. The API can be found at `http://api.jquery.com/jQuery.ajax/`. In the following example, we are simply going to log a message to the console before the AJAX request is made to our server:

```
$('.show-popup').fancybox({
  ajax: {
    beforeSend: function(xhr) {
      console.log("About to send a request with XHR object: ",
        xhr);
    }
  }
});
```

The given code will log a message to the console and the jQuery XHR object that represents the request. For more details on the jQuery XHR object, see the jQuery AJAX API page's link mentioned previously.

Now, anytime Fancybox is about to make our AJAX request, the function set in the `beforeSend` property will run. This is one of the many properties that can be set in the AJAX object; the full list is provided in the jQuery API at the link mentioned previously.

Loading additional types of content (Intermediate)

Fancybox can load more than just YouTube videos, images, and asynchronous content. The three content types we are going to cover in this recipe are SWF (flash files), inline, and iframe. We have already discussed the iframe content type to some extent when we loaded a YouTube video into Fancybox. However, iframes can contain more than just YouTube videos, so we will discuss some of the settings that are useful when using iframe content.

Getting ready

Before we start loading these different types of content, we'll need to find an SWF file. There is one included in the code examples; so if you need one, you can use that one. This is the file that I will be using in the instructions of this recipe. We will be creating a page with a link to each type of content in the order SWF, inline, and iframe.

How to do it...

1. Add three links to the `index.html` file. We need one for the SWF file, one for `inline` content, and one for an iframe content, shown as follows:

   ```
   <a class="show-popup" data-fancybox-type="swf" href="demo.
   swf">Flash File(SWF)</a>
   <a class="show-popup" data-fancybox-type="inline"
   href="#inline">Inline Content</a>
   <a class="show-popup" data-fancybox-type="iframe" href="">iFrame
   Content</a>
   ```

   In the given code, we have an anchor tag for each content type. The first one is for the SWF file, which has the `href` attribute populated with the filename of the SWF file to use. The second is for the `inline` content, and the third is for the iframe content.

2. Put the SWF file in the same directory as the `index.html` file. In the example code, the file is called `demo.swf`, but you can call it whatever you like.

3. The `scripts.js` file should have a call to Fancybox on the `show-popup` class, shown as follows:

```
$('.show-popup').fancybox();
```

4. The **Flash File** link should now work with Fancybox. If you click on it, you should see your SWF file displayed in the Fancybox pop up. The `demo.swf` file included with the code examples is just the **Fancybox Flash Demo** text bouncing around a white stage, as shown in the following screenshot:

5. Next up is the `inline` content. First, we need to add some `inline` content to the page that we want Fancybox to load. Let's just add some simple HTML:

```
<div id="inline">
  <h2>Some Inline Content!</h2>
  <p>With some simple text as well!</p>
</div>
```

The HTML code we are adding is a `div` tag with an ID of `inline` and the `div` tag contains some basic HTML contents. This content can be added anywhere inside the `body` tag of the `index.html` file.

6. Next we need to make sure that our link is correct. The `href` attribute of the `inline` link should be `#inline`. Note that `inline` is the ID of our `div` tag and is how Fancybox identifies the content it needs to grab from the HTML file. You should now see the contents of the `div` tag with the ID of `inline` displayed in Fancybox.

 Fancybox will automatically hide the inline HTML that it shows when the pop up is closed. In the *There's more...* section, we will cover how to prevent this from happening.

7. Any external website can be loaded with the `iframe` option in Fancybox. For this example, we're going to load the Fancybox website at `http://fancyapps.com/fancybox/`.

8. Our last link already has the `data-fancybox-type` attribute set to `iframe`, so we just have to add the Fancybox website URL to the `href` attribute of the anchor tag as follows:

```
<a class="show-popup" data-fancybox-type="iframe"
  href="http://fancyapps.com/fancybox/">iFrame Content</a>
```

You should see the Fancybox website loaded in the Fancybox pop up.

9. All three links should continue to work on the page.

How it works...

Fancybox provides functionality for properly loading most of the common types of website content. For SWF files, it creates the appropriate HTML and uses the file provided in the `href` attribute. For inline content, it moves the content with the ID provided into the Fancybox `div` tag and replaces it with a placeholder string. Then, when Fancybox is closed, it knows where to put the content back on the page. For the iframe content, it relies on the functionality of iframes in web browsers to properly render the content from the URL provided in the `href` attribute of the link.

There's more...

There isn't much extra that Fancybox can do with these less common forms of content. However, some of the functionality regarding inline content may require some additional work to get the desired effect.

Showing inline content after closing Fancybox

As mentioned earlier, Fancybox likes to hide inline content once it has been shown in the Fancybox pop up. Fortunately, we can rely on one of the callback methods to make our content visible after Fancybox has closed. The method we will be using is `afterClose`. Let's make the inline content from step 5 display after Fancybox has been closed:

1. We're going to expand on the inline functionality used earlier. Open the `scripts.js` file and add an object to the Fancybox call that has the `afterClose` setting.

2. Define the `afterClose` setting as a function, which shows the content using the jQuery `.show()` method:

```
$('.show-popup').fancybox({
  afterClose: function() {
    this.content.show();
  }
});
```

The `this` keyword in the `afterClose` function is the Fancybox object that is being used to show the content. It has a property called `content`, which is the content that the Fancybox pop up is configured to display. In this case, the `content` property is the `div` tag with an ID of `inline`. When we call the `show()` method on it, jQuery adds the `display: block` style to the `div` tag.

The inline content should now be displayed on the page when the Fancybox pop up is closed.

Adding thumbnails to a gallery (Simple)

Fancybox provides the ability to have a thumbnails display under an image gallery. Let's take a look at getting the thumbnails displayed under our image gallery.

Getting ready

We're going to use the image gallery that we already created in the *Creating an image gallery* recipe. If you don't have yours available, you can find a simple image gallery in the example code.

How to do it...

1. Remember all of those extra files that come with the Fancybox download? We need to add the stylesheet and JavaScript files necessary for the thumbnails to work. In the `head` tag of our `index.html` file, add the following two lines:

```
<link rel="stylesheet"
  href="fancybox/source/helpers/jquery.fancybox-
  thumbs.css?v=1.0.7" type="text/css" media="screen" />
<script type="text/javascript"
  src="fancybox/source/helpers/jquery.fancybox-
  thumbs.js?v=1.0.7"></script>
```

We have now loaded the necessary files for the thumbnails helper. Helpers are supplemental functionality to the Fancybox plugin. They aren't required for the plugin to work but they can provide some great additional functionalities.

2. Next, we need to tell Fancybox to use the thumbnails helper. We do that by passing the Fancybox call a setting as follows:

```
$('.fancybox').fancybox({
  helpers: {
    thumbs: {
      width: 75,
      height: 50
    }
  }
});
```

3. In the given code, we are calling Fancybox with a `helpers` setting, which has a `thumbs` property that has two properties: `width` and `height`. The `width` and `height` properties define the width and height of the displayed thumbnails. You should now see the thumbnails along the bottom of your window as shown in the following screenshot:

How it works...

The thumbnails helper creates image tags along the bottom of the screen, which contain the same images that will be displayed as part of the gallery. It simply constrains the height and width of the images using CSS. When you click on an image, the helper takes you to the gallery of that image and adjusts the positioning of the thumbnails.

There's more...

The thumbnails helper has a few settings that we can use to adjust its positioning as well as the way it determines the source of the thumbnail images. We're also going to take a look at applying styles to the thumbnails to adjust their positioning in the window.

Changing the thumbnail source

The thumbnail sources are, by default, the exact same images as the large ones. By using the exact same images, the load times of the thumbnails will be significantly greater and the thumbnails will require considerably more bandwidth. Let's take a look at adjusting the location of our thumbnails. We can use the source setting of the thumbnails helper to provide a function, which provides the URL for each image's thumbnail. Let's change the source of the thumbnails for the image gallery:

1. In the `index.html` file, add the `data-thumbnail` attribute to each image. The value should be the thumbnail you want to use for the image, shown as follows:

```
<a class="fancybox" rel="gallery" data-
   thumbnail="images/frozen-lake-sm.png"
   href="images/frozen-lake.png">Frozen Lake</a>
```

2. Add the `source` property to the thumbnails settings object:

```
source: function(image) {
   return $(image.element).data("thumbnail");
}
```

3. Have the function return the URL that matches this image's thumbnail. In this case, it should return the `data-thumbnail` attribute's value, which we get by using the jQuery `data` method and telling it that we want to get the `thumbnail` data item, or the `data-thumbnail` attribute, shown as follows:

```
$('.fancybox').fancybox({
  helpers: {
    thumbs: {
      width: 75,
      height: 50,
      source: function(image) {
        return $(image.element).data("thumbnail");
      }
    }
  }
});
```

The call to Fancybox should now look something like the given code, with all of our settings being passed in.

Positioning the thumbnails

The thumbnails can be positioned to either the top or the bottom of the screen. The default is to have the thumbnails at the bottom of the screen, but if you want to make them visible at the top of the screen, simply add the `position` property to the `thumbs` settings object, shown as follows:

```
$('.fancybox').fancybox({
  helpers: {
    thumbs: {
      width: 75,
      height: 50,
      source: function(image) {
        return $(image.element).data("thumbnail");
      },
      position: 'top'
    }
  }
});
```

With the `position: 'top'` setting applied, you should see the thumbnails along the top of the window.

Showing hidden content

What if we want the inline content to only show up in the Fancybox pop up? This can be done with simple CSS. All we have to do is make the `div` tag with the ID of `inline` have a `style` tag of `display: none`. In the `head` tag at the top of the `index.html` page, add a `style` block as follows:

```
<style type="text/css">
  #inline {
    display: none;
  }
</style>
```

This `style` block applies the `display: none` CSS to any element with an ID of `inline`. We also need to undo the function that we defined in the earlier section, so make sure that the Fancybox call on the `show-popup` links is back to:

```
$('.show-popup').fancybox();
```

Now, the content should be hidden when the page loads, visible in the Fancybox pop up, and hidden once Fancybox closes.

Adding buttons to image slideshows (Simple)

Another helper that Fancybox provides is the slideshow buttons. The buttons allow the user to go back and forward, play and pause, and close the Fancybox pop up from a simple bar of buttons.

Getting ready

Like the thumbnails helper, we will need to include the JavaScript and stylesheet files for the buttons helper.

How to do it...

1. Add the stylesheet and JavaScript tags to the `head` tag of the `index.html` file, shown as follows:

```
<link rel="stylesheet"
  href="fancybox/source/helpers/jquery.fancybox-
  buttons.css?v=1.0.5" type="text/css" media="screen" />
<script type="text/javascript"
  src="fancybox/source/helpers/jquery.fancybox-
  buttons.js?v=1.0.5"></script>
```

Next, we need to add the `buttons` option to the settings for Fancybox:

```
$('.fancybox').fancybox({
  helpers: {
    buttons: {}
  }
});
```

Here, we have set the `helpers` option with a property of `buttons`, which is an empty object. We have to provide an object for the `buttons` option otherwise it will not work, so we provide Fancybox with an empty object because we are not setting any property on `buttons` themselves.

2. You should now see and be able to use the buttons at the top of the page.

How it works...

The buttons are HTML links that call some of the API methods provided by the Fancybox plugin when clicked.

There's more...

The buttons can have two settings defined for them, the `tpl` (template) to use to create them and the `position` property, which is used to position the buttons.

Changing the position of the buttons

The position setting allows us to tell the buttons whether to position them along the top or the bottom of the screen. By default, the buttons display along the top of the screen. If we set the `position` property of the `buttons` settings object to be `bottom`, then the buttons will be displayed along the bottom of the screen.

```
$('.fancybox').fancybox({
  helpers: {
    buttons: {
      position: 'bottom'
    }
  }
});
```

Here, we have set the `position` property of the `buttons` settings object to be `bottom`, so our buttons will be displayed along the bottom of the screen.

Adjusting the HTML template

The Fancybox buttons helper allows us to provide an HTML template to render the buttons. The default buttons use a template as in the following code:

```
<div id="fancybox-buttons" class="bottom special">
<ul>
<li><a class="btnPrev" title="Previous"
  href="javascript:;"></a></li>
<li><a class="btnPlay" title="Start slideshow"
  href="javascript:;"></a></li>
<li><a class="btnNext" title="Next" href="javascript:;"></a></li>
<li><a class="btnToggle" title="Toggle size"
  href="javascript:;"></a></li>
<li><a class="btnClose" title="Close"
  onclick="jQuery.fancybox.close()"></a></li>
</ul>
</div>
```

I would recommend starting with the default button template and modifying it if you want to adjust the template at all. I would also recommend changing the template by using an HTML element on the page using the following steps:

1. Create the template on the page inside the `index.html` file, shown as follows:

    ```
    <div class="hidden">
    <div id="fancybox-buttons" class="bottom
      special"><ul><li><a class="btnPrev" title="Previous"
      href="javascript:;"></a></li><li><a class="btnPlay"
      title="Start slideshow"
      href="javascript:;"></a></li><li><a class="btnNext"
      title="Next" href="javascript:;"></a></li><li><a
      class="btnToggle" title="Toggle size"
      href="javascript:;"></a></li><li><a class="btnClose"
      title="Close"
      href="javascript:jQuery.fancybox.close();"></a>
      </li></ul></div>
    </div>
    ```

    Note that in the example, we placed the `fancybox-buttons` div inside the `div` tag with the `hidden` class, which makes it such that the buttons are not displayed on the page until Fancybox is displayed.

2. Retrieve the element from the page via jQuery and set it into the `tpl` setting, shown as follows:

```
$('.fancybox').fancybox({
  helpers: {
    buttons: {
      position: 'bottom',
      tpl: $('#fancybox-buttons')
    }
  }
});
```

In the previous code, we have set the `tpl` property of the `buttons` settings object to be the entire `fancybox-buttons` div, which we have retrieved from the HTML document via jQuery.

Customizing other helpers (Intermediate)

The image title and transparent overlay are also Fancybox helpers. Unlike the other helpers that we have been working with, these are included in the default application. Each of these helpers has a few settings that we can use.

Getting ready

The title has only one setting, the `type` setting. The `type` setting of the title determines where it positions on the image. The overlay has five settings: `closeClick`, `speedOut`, `showEarly`, `css`, and `locked`. We will adjust all of these settings to see how it impacts the functionality of Fancybox.

How to do it...

1. Change the title helper's `type` setting to be `over`.

```
$('.fancybox').fancybox({
  helpers: {
    title: {
      type: 'over'
    }
  }
});
```

The `type` setting for the title can also be `float`, `inside`, and `over`. The default option is `float`. You can change the `type` setting to be whichever you prefer; I would recommend trying all of them and seeing which one you like best. You can also turn off the title by setting the title setting to `null`:

```
$('.fancybox').fancybox({
  helpers: {
    title: null
  }
});
```

2. Change the overlay helper's `closeClick` setting to `false`.

   The `closeClick` setting allows the user to click the overlay to close the Fancybox pop up when it is set to `true`. If it is set to `false`, clicking on the overlay does nothing.

3. Change the `speedOut` setting to `1000`.

   The `speedOut` setting determines how quickly the overlay should disappear. The number provided is the time in milliseconds that the animation will take, so in our case the overlay will disappear in one second (1000 milliseconds).

4. Change the `showEarly` setting to be `false`.

   The `showEarly` setting will display the overlay immediately if it is set to `true`. If it is set to `false`, the overlay will only show once the content is loaded in the Fancybox pop up.

5. Change the `locked` setting to `false`.

   The `locked` setting will prevent the content from showing a scrollbar when displaying a Fancybox pop up. I would recommend leaving this set to `true` at all times, so that the user cannot scroll while Fancybox is displaying. Allowing the user to scroll while Fancybox is displaying could result in the user not seeing the Fancybox pop up at all.

   With all of these settings applied, our call to Fancybox looks like the following code:

```
$('.fancybox').fancybox({
  helpers: {
    overlay: {
      closeClick: false,
      speedOut: 1000,
      showEarly: false,
      locked: false
    }
  }
});
```

And now we have a Fancybox pop that cannot be clicked on to close the overlay, takes one second to animate back to being hidden, does not show the overlay until the content finishes loading, and does not lock the window size to the overlay area.

6. It is also possible to turn off the overlay entirely by setting it to null, similar to the title:

```
$('.fancybox').fancybox({
  helpers: {
    overlay: null
  }
});
```

How it works...

Fancybox provides us with a range of settings that we can configure for the overlay. We can also adjust the positioning of the title for our images. This functionality is all built into the Fancybox plugin.

There's more...

The other setting that is provided for the overlay is `css`. This setting allows us to define specific styles that we want to use on the overlay.

Adding CSS to the overlay

The overlay `css` setting is useful for applying custom styles to the overlay. A simple one is instead of a black transparent overlay, we want a white transparent overlay. We can use the `css` setting to apply the background style to the overlay, shown as follows:

```
$('.fancybox').fancybox({
  helpers: {
    overlay: {
      css: {
        background: "rgba(255, 255, 255, 0.7)"
      }
    }
  }
});
```

In the given code, we have provided the `css` property on the overlay settings object with a background of `rgba(255, 255, 255, 0.7)`, which is the equivalent of a white background at 70 percent opacity. Styles are applied using the same object structure that would be passed to the jQuery `css` method.

Modifying styles and layout (Intermediate)

Now that we have a basic handle on how Fancybox works and some of the things it can do, let's start looking at modifying the way the Fancybox pop up looks. Fancybox provides a number of useful settings we can use to change the way that the Fancybox pop up looks. We're going to start with the basic margin and height settings and work our way to the auto-sizing settings.

Getting ready

To get things started, we just need a simple Fancybox pop up. In the example code, I have copied the code from the *Fancybox with a single image* recipe, where we used Fancybox to load a single image.

How to do it...

1. The Fancybox margins indicate the minimum distance between the Fancybox pop up and the edge of the window. To change the margins of the Fancybox pop up, we provide it a number. This sets all of the margins to be the same, as shown in the following code:

```
$('#show-fancybox').fancybox({
  margin: 50
});
```

You can also set the margins individually by using an array. The order of the values in the array is as follows: [top, right, bottom, left]. For example, say we wanted to have the margin on the left higher than the margin on the right, as shown in the following code:

```
$('#show-fancybox').fancybox({
  margin: [50, 50, 50, 200]
});
```

Now the Fancybox pop up will be, at minimum, 200 pixels from the left edge of the window. The default margin is 20 pixels.

2. Padding is the space inside the Fancybox pop up between the edge of the pop up and the content. Padding can be set exactly the same way as margins: either as a number that determines the padding on all sides, or as an array that sets the padding on each side individually. If we did not want any padding, we would set it as shown in the following code:

```
$('#show-fancybox').fancybox({
  padding: 0
});
```

The default padding value is 20 pixels.

3. Fancybox can be told whether or not we want it to automatically size to the content we provide. If we set the `autoSize` setting to `false`, the Fancybox pop up will become the default height and width. Note that the `autoSize` setting does not apply to images; it only applies to every other type of content that Fancybox will display. The default setting for `autoSize` is `true`.

We can also provide the height and width for the Fancybox pop up. However, these two properties only work with the iframe and SWF content, unless we set the `autoSize` setting to `false`. Let's set the `autoSize` setting to `false`, the `height` to `300`, and the `width` to `200` and load the Fancybox website in the Fancybox pop up, as shown in the following code:

```
$('#show-fancybox').fancybox({
    padding: 0,
    autoSize: false,
    height: 300,
    width: 250
});
```

Here we have set the padding to `0`, the `autoSize` setting to `false`, the `height` to `300`, and the `width` to `200`. This results in a very small window that has loaded the Fancybox website, as seen in the following screenshot:

The default height setting is `600` pixels and the default width setting is `800` pixels.

4. Fancybox also provides the `minWidth`, `minHeight`, `maxWidth`, and `maxHeight` settings. These settings do exactly what one would expect them to do: set the minimum or maximum height and width of the Fancybox pop up. Note that setting maximums and minimums does apply to images, so if you need to specify the height or width of the pop up that displays images, the following settings are the ones to use:

```
$('#show-fancybox').fancybox({
    padding: 0,
    maxHeight: 400,
    maxWidth: 300,
    minHeight: 250,
    minWidth: 250
});
```

In the previous code, we set a maximum height of 400 pixels, a maximum width of 300 pixels, a minimum width of 300 pixels, and a minimum width of 250 pixels. This allows the images we load to still scale if they need to, but only within the limits we have provided.

The default minimum height and width is 100 pixels and the default maximum height and width is 9999 pixels.

5. Fancybox automatically resizes and repositions the Fancybox window when it is resized. Because we are showing images, we want it to stay the size it is no matter how the window resizes. We can use the `autoResize` and `autoCenter` settings to prevent or allow resizing when the window resizes, as shown in the following code:

```
$('#show-fancybox').fancybox({
autoResize: false,
autoCenter: false
});
```

Now that we have set `autoResize` and `autoCenter` to `false`, the Fancybox pop up will not reposition or resize when the window is resized.

The default value for both of these settings is `!isTouch`. Fancybox has a variable defined inside of it, which identifies touch devices, and prevents resizing and auto-centering on touch devices.

6. The last setting to discuss is the `fitToView` setting. The `fitToView` setting will make the Fancybox pop up resize to fit inside the window when it is opened. Going along with the settings we have set in step 5, we probably don't want the window to resize when it is opened for the first time. We set `fitToView` to `false`, as shown in the following code:

```
$('#show-fancybox').fancybox({
    autoResize: false,
    autoCenter: false,
    fitToView: false
});
```

7. Now when Fancybox is first opened, the window is the size we have set it to be, instead of attempting to resize it to fit the browser. The default value of the `fitToView` setting is `true`.

How it works...

When Fancybox first opens up, it identifies the size of the window and the size of the content it is loading. Next, it checks the settings we have provided to see how it needs to size the content to fit the parameters we have defined. After it has determined the appropriate height, width, margins, and padding to use for the Fancybox pop up, it applies them via the `style` attribute on the Fancybox pop up div.

Changing slideshow settings (Advanced)

Let's take a look at the settings that Fancybox exposes us to for image slideshows. We can change the speed of the slideshow, whether or not it will automatically begin playing when it is opened, whether or not it will loop, and what image should be displayed first.

Getting ready

We're going to use the same image gallery we have been using throughout the book. You can find the code for this recipe in the `Changing slideshow settings` folder in the code bundle.

How to do it...

1. The first setting we are going to adjust is the speed of the slideshow. The speed can be changed by adjusting the `playSpeed` setting. The speed is the duration that an image will stay on the slideshow (in milliseconds). The speed can be set by using the following code:

```
$('.fancybox').fancybox({
  playSpeed: 1000
});
```

Here we are setting the `playSpeed` setting to `1000`, which will mean that each image will stay on the screen for only one second (1000 milliseconds). The default `playSpeed` is 3000 milliseconds.

2. Now that we have the slideshow playing faster, let's make it play immediately after Fancybox displays the images. The `autoPlay` setting allows us to do exactly that.

```
$('.fancybox').fancybox({
  playSpeed: 1000,
  autoPlay: true
});
```

Now we are setting `playSpeed` to be 1000 milliseconds and we are setting `autoPlay` to `true`, which will make the slideshow play as soon as Fancybox opens. The `autoPlay` setting defaults to `false`.

3. Right now our slideshow will start over when it reaches the last image in the gallery. If we want it to stop when it reaches the last image we can set the `loop` setting to `false`.

```
$('.fancybox').fancybox({
  playSpeed: 1000,
  autoPlay: true,
  loop: false
});
```

Now that we have `loop` set to `false` our slideshow will stop with the last image. The default value for the `loop` setting is `true`.

4. Fancybox also allows us to set the number of images to preload when the gallery is opened via the `preload` setting. The `preload` setting takes the number of images for Fancybox preload. Since our gallery is small, let's just have Fancybox preload all four images.

```
$('.fancybox').fancybox({
  playSpeed: 1000,
  autoPlay: true,
  loop: false,
  preload: 4
});
```

Now Fancybox will preload all four of our images for the slideshow. The default value for the `preload` setting is 3.

How it works...

All of the settings we looked at previously are used by default in Fancybox. When we adjust the settings they are actually being overridden. If you would like more information on how the settings for jQuery plugins work, I would recommend looking into the `jQuery.fn.extend()` function. You can find the details on the jQuery API site at `http://api.jquery.com/jQuery.fn.extend/`. The `jQuery.fn.extend()` method is the accepted and the most common way to write jQuery plugins.

There's more...

There are a few other settings we can change for slideshows. They are considerably less useful than the other settings, but they may be important to know.

The index setting

The `index` setting is used to specify the image that the gallery will start on by default. This setting only applies when the slideshow is triggered manually. Triggering Fancybox manually is as simple as calling the `$.fancybox.open()` function. This function takes an array of JavaScript objects that represent images and creates a Fancybox slideshow from them. This would look like the following code:

```
$(document).ready(function() {
$(".fancybox").click(function() {
  $.fancybox.open([
      {href:"images/waterfall.png"},
      {href:"images/frozen-lake.png"},
      {href:"images/road-in-forest.png"},
      {href:"images/boston.png"}
    ],
    {
    index: 2
  });
});
});
```

Here we are listening for the `click` event on the link with the class of `fancybox`. When the link is clicked on, we are telling Fancybox to open manually and providing it with an array of images to load as part of our slideshow. We are then specifying the `index` to start at 2. Since we provided an `index` of 2, the slideshow will start on the third image (the slideshow index is zero based).

The direction setting

The `direction` setting allows us to tell Fancybox from which direction the next or previous image should animate into view. The default for next is `left` and previous is `right`. We can change them to be the opposite using the `direction` setting, as shown in the following code:

```
$('.fancybox').fancybox({
  playSpeed: 1000,
  autoPlay: true,
  direction: {
    next: 'right',
    prev: 'left'
  }
});
```

Now the next image will slide in from the right and the previous image will slide in from the left.

Adding custom styles (Intermediate)

Let's take a look at customizing the look of Fancybox even beyond the basic settings that we have covered previously. Now we're going to cover the `wrapCSS` setting as well as how to adjust the CSS of the default HTML that Fancybox uses.

Getting ready

Let's start by adding a CSS file to our HTML. Create a file called `styles.css` and put it in the same directory as the `index.html` file. Include the `styles.css` file on the page using a `link` tag:

```
<link rel="stylesheet" type="text/css" href="styles.css">
```

Now that we have the `styles.css` file created and loaded on the page, we can use it for all of the styles we want to add to our page.

How to do it...

1. To start out we'll look at the `wrapCSS` setting. Fancybox adds whatever classes you pass to this setting to the top-most div of the Fancybox pop up. For this example, we want Fancybox to add the `custom-stuff` class to the wrapping div.

   ```
   $('.fancybox').fancybox({
           wrapCSS: "custom-stuff"
   });
   ```

   Now if we open a browser and inspect the Fancybox wrapping div, we should see our class added to the div.

   ```
   <div class="fancybox-wrap fancybox-desktop fancybox
     -type-image custom-stuff fancybox-opened
       " tabindex="-1" style="width: 622px; height
         : auto; position: absolute; top: 225px; left
           : 20px; opacity: 1; overflow: visible;">
   ```

   In the previous div, we have all of the Fancybox classes and attributes on the Fancybox wrapping div, as well as the `custom-stuff` class we added. Fancybox creates the div with several classes and styles included. The classes are used to provide the default style for Fancybox and are inside the `jquery.fancybox.css` file. The styles that are added are determined from the settings that are passed to Fancybox. If no settings are provided, then the height and width are set based on the content, and the top and left values are set to position Fancybox at the middle of the screen. We covered adjusting the positioning and sizing of Fancybox in the *Modifying styles and layout* recipe.

2. Now that we have our `custom-stuff` class added, we can use it to customize the styles in the Fancybox pop up div. In the `styles.css` file, you can add whatever styles you would like to add to the pop up. For this example, we want all of the images to have a box shadow and a small green border.

```
.custom-stuff img {
  border: 3px solid green;
  -webkit-box-shadow: 0px 9px 16px -6px #000;
  box-shadow: 0px 9px 16px -6px #000;
}
```

Vendor prefixes (such as `-webkit-`) have become a common way for browsers to introduce new features before the official specification is released. In this case, we are only using the `-webkit-` prefix because Firefox has supported the official specification since Version 4.0, while the iOS Safari browser just received official support as iOS 6.

Now we should see our styles applied to the images. In this case, we'll see a green border and a shadow underneath the image, as shown in the following screenshot:

How it works...

The `wrapCSS` property adds the class you provide it to the Fancybox wrapping div. We can then use this class to select elements inside Fancybox and apply styles to them. The advantage of using the `wrapCSS` setting to add a class is that if we wanted to target the Fancybox wrapping div directly, we can override the default settings, which are set via several of the classes that Fancybox uses such as `fancybox-opened`, `fancybox-wrap`, and `fancybox-desktop`. We can do this using CSS to select our class and the class we want to override: `.fancybox-opened.custom-stuff`.

Changing animation effects (Intermediate)

Fancybox allows us to change all of the settings for the various animations it does. Let's talk about changing these settings and its impact on the Fancybox pop up.

Getting ready

We're going to continue to use the gallery we used in the previous recipe. Fancybox uses the jQuery animation effects to produce its animations. This means that all of the animations have three basic pieces: effect, easing, and duration. The effect is the name of the animation effect that we want Fancybox to use. Easing is the curve that represents the speed throughout the duration of the animation. Duration is the amount of time the animation will take to complete. We will look at changing all of these settings for Fancybox. To learn more about jQuery animation check out the jQuery API at `http://api.jquery.com/animate/`.

How to do it...

1. Let's make our Fancybox take a whole second to display and close. We can do this using the `openSpeed` and `closeSpeed` settings. All of the animation durations are in milliseconds.

```
$('.fancybox').fancybox({
   openSpeed: 1000,
   closeSpeed: 1000
});
```

Now our Fancybox pop up will take one second (1000 milliseconds) to open and close. The default for these settings is 250 milliseconds.

2. We can also set the speed that it takes to switch between images using the `nextSpeed` and `prevSpeed` settings. Let's make this transition also take 1000 milliseconds, as shown in the following code:

```
$('.fancybox').fancybox({
    openSpeed: 1000,
    closeSpeed: 1000,
    nextSpeed: 1000,
    prevSpeed: 1000
});
```

Now all of our animations will take an entire second to run. The default for these settings is also 250 milliseconds.

3. Next let's look at changing the effect that Fancybox uses to open and close. To change the effect, we use the `openEffect` and `closeEffect` settings. We have three options to select from: `fade`, `elastic`, and `none`. The default option is `fade`, which makes Fancybox fade in and out when it is opened and closed. That's pretty boring, so let's use `elastic` instead.

```
$('.fancybox').fancybox({
    openSpeed: 1000,
    closeSpeed: 1000,
    nextSpeed: 1000,
    prevSpeed: 1000,
    openEffect: 'elastic',
    closeEffect: 'elastic'
});
```

Now the Fancybox pop up starts small and expands. We can also set the effect to `none`, which turns the animation off.

4. We can also apply these same effects to the animations between images in the slideshow. Let's make the transition between images just fade in and out. By default, Fancybox uses `elastic` for the image transitions. We use the `nextEffect` and `prevEffect` settings to change the effect of the next and previous image animations, as shown in the following code:

```
$('.fancybox').fancybox({
    openSpeed: 1000,
    closeSpeed: 1000,
    nextSpeed: 1000,
    prevSpeed: 1000,
    openEffect: 'elastic',
    closeEffect: 'elastic',
    nextEffect: 'fade',
    prevEffect: 'fade'
});
```

Now the transition between images in the slideshow will just be a simple fade in and out. You can also set these settings to `none`, which will just switch the images without any animation.

5.   The last setting to change is easing. We can change easing for the different animations in the exact same way as the previous two settings. We can change the open and close easing using `openEasing` and `closeEasing`. We can change the next and previous easing using `nextEasing` and `prevEasing`. Let's change these to use the `linear` easing curve, as shown in the following code:

```
$('.fancybox').fancybox({
    openSpeed: 1000,
    closeSpeed: 1000,
    nextSpeed: 1000,
    prevSpeed: 1000,
    openEffect: 'elastic',
    closeEffect: 'elastic',
    nextEffect: 'fade',
    prevEffect: 'fade',
    openEasing: 'linear',
    closeEasing: 'linear',
    nextEasing: 'linear',
    prevEasing: 'linear'
});
```

Now our animation will have no easing. Using the `linear` easing curve means that our animation speed will be constant throughout the entire duration of the animation. These two, `linear` and `swing`, are the only two easing curves available in standard jQuery.

How it works...

Animations are complex beasts and the animations available as part of Fancybox can be customized quite well. Speed and effect are fairly straightforward; the more difficult concept is easing. If you are unsure about adjusting easing, I would recommend against changing this setting. The default option of `swing` is a very natural easing curve (slow to fast to slow is exactly how most things move in real life and is what the swing curve does). If you are looking for more easing curves, I would recommend looking at jQuery UI at `http://jqueryui.com/`, which introduces a handful of additional easing curves. The default easing curve for all Fancybox effects is `swing`.

Changing keyboard shortcuts (Advanced)

Fancybox allows users to navigate through an image slideshow with keyboard shortcuts. Let's take a look at changing these from the default settings.

Getting ready

Fancybox relies on jQuery `keypress` events to determine which key was pressed. Each key is identified by a number that is its charCode. A key's charCode can be found by looking it up on `http://www.cambiaresearch.com/articles/15/javascript-char-codes-key-codes`. For more information about retrieving charCodes from jQuery, see `http://api.jquery.com/category/events/event-object/` and look at the `event.which` documentation.

We can change or add `keybindings` for these actions: `next`, `previous`, `close`, `play`, and `toggle fullscreen`. We're going to make the *W*, *A*, *S*, and *D* keys work for next/previous functionality; - to close; *Enter* to play; and + for fullscreen.

How to do it...

1. Let's start with making the *W*, *A*, *S*, and *D* keys work for next/previous. We want to keep the default keyboard shortcuts, so we must copy the default options from the Fancybox API page. To start with, our call to Fancybox will look just like the default options:

```
$('.fancybox').fancybox({
  keys: {
    next : {
      13 : 'left', // enter
      34 : 'up',   // page down
      39 : 'left', // right arrow
      40 : 'up'    // down arrow
    },
    prev : {
       8 : 'right', // backspace
      33 : 'down',  // page up
      37 : 'right', // left arrow
      38 : 'down'   // up arrow
    },
    close  : [27], // escape key
    play   : [32], // space - start/stop slideshow
    toggle : [70]  // letter "f" - toggle fullscreen
  }
});
```

2. Now we have an exact copy of the default settings for our keyboard shortcuts. All we have to do now is look up the character codes for the keys we want and add them to the appropriate spots in the settings. Note that we want to assign *W* for the up action, *S* for the down action, *A* for the left action, and *D* for the right action. The action directions are relative to the current image's location inside the gallery. This means that if our gallery had nine images in a three-by-three grid, we can move from the top-left corner image to the top-center image by pressing *D*. We can move from there to the center image by pressing *S*. The other actions can move around the image gallery in the same fashion. The character codes for the keys are as follows: *W* is 87, *A* is 65, *S* is 83, and *D* is 68. If we add these keys to our keys setting, it will look like the following code:

```
$('.fancybox').fancybox({
  keys: {
    next : {
        13 : 'left', // enter
        34 : 'up',   // page down
        39 : 'left', // right arrow
        40 : 'up',   // down arrow
        68 : 'left', // "D" key
        83 : 'up'    // "S" key
    },
    prev : {
        8  : 'right',  // backspace
        33 : 'down',   // page up
        37 : 'right',  // left arrow
        38 : 'down',   // up arrow
        65 : 'right',  // "A" key
        87 : 'down',   // "W" key
    },
    close  : [27], // escape key
    play   : [32], // space - start/stop slideshow
    toggle : [70]  // letter "f" - toggle fullscreen
  }
});
```

We have added the *D* and *S* keys to the next setting, with *D* set to left and *S* set to up. We have added the *A* and *W* keys to the prev setting, with *A* set to right and *W* set to down. Now our *W*, *A*, *S*, and *D* keys will move the images around in the slideshow just like the arrows.

3. Next we will set the - key to close the pop up. Because the close setting is just an array, it is as simple as adding the charCode for the - key to the array. The charCode for the - key is 189, so we can change the close setting to be as follows:

```
close : [27, 189], // escape key and "-" key
```

4. The next `keypress` we want to bind to is the *Enter* key. Note that the *Enter* key right now is bound inside the `next` setting, so we'll have to remove it from there, and then add it to the `play` setting, as shown in the following code:

```
play : [32, 13],  // space and enter - start/stop slideshow
```

5. The last key we want to bind to is the + key, which we will use to toggle the fullscreen mode. The charCode for + is `187`.

```
toggle : [70, 187]  // letter "f"
  and "+" key - toggle fullscreen
```

6. Now all of our new key shortcuts will work and the defaults (except for *Enter*) will work as well. The whole call to Fancybox will now look as follows:

```
$('.fancybox').fancybox({
  keys: {
    next : {
        34 : 'up',    // page down
        39 : 'left', // right arrow
        40 : 'up',    // down arrow
        68 : 'left', // "D" key
        83 : 'up'    // "S" key
    },
    prev : {
        8  : 'right',  // backspace
        33 : 'down',   // page up
        37 : 'right',  // left arrow
        38 : 'down',   // up arrow
        65 : 'right',  // "A" key
        87 : 'down'       // "W" key
    },
    close  : [27, 189], // escape key and "-" key
    play   : [32, 13],  //
      space and enter - start/stop slideshow
    toggle : [70, 187]  //
      letter "f" and "+" key - toggle fullscreen
  }
});
```

How it works...

Fancybox binds to the `keydown` event, which is fired from jQuery when the user presses the down arrow key. Fancybox then compares the charCode passed from the `keydown` event to the settings we defined in the previous code and determines the action to take based on that charCode, if any.

Interacting with Fancybox (Advanced)

Fancybox provides a number of methods that we can use to programmatically interact with the Fancybox pop up. Let's take a look at some of these methods and at what they allow us to do.

Getting ready

To make things simple, we are just going to use a single-image pop up like the one found in the *Installing Fancybox* recipe. We'll be looking at the pieces of the API that allow us to interact with just the Fancybox pop up in this recipe. We'll cover manually opening and closing Fancybox, the update and toggle functions, the reposition function, the show and hide loader functions, and the close function.

How to do it...

1. Let's start with opening the Fancybox pop up using the API. We used this briefly in the recipe on changing slideshow settings. The method is $.fancybox.open and can be passed a range of different parameters. The first parameter is the content to open inside of Fancybox and the second parameter is the options we want to use for this Fancybox pop up. If we want to open Fancybox using the API method and have it do the exact same thing as in the *Fancybox with a single image* recipe, we'll call Fancybox and pass it the href tag of the image as shown in the following code:

```
$('#show-fancybox').click(function() {
  $.fancybox.open('images/waterfall.png');
});
```

The previous code uses a jQuery click event binding, which is passed an anonymous function, to tell Fancybox to open and use the string we provided to open. The string can be a range of different types of content that Fancybox can open. If you wanted it to open an image gallery, images can be passed in as an array, as shown in the code:

```
$('#show-fancybox').click(function() {
  $.fancybox.open([
    {href:'images/waterfall.png'},
    {href:'images/frozen-lake.png'}
  ]);
});
```

The objects can contain the href and title tags for the image, as shown in the following code:

```
{href:'images/frozen-lake.png', title: "Frozen Lake"}
```

For the remainder of this recipe, we will have Fancybox load some HTML. Add this HTML to the `index.html` file inside the body:

```
<div id="fancybox-content" class="hidden">
  <h2>Super Simple Fancybox Popup</h2>
  <p>With some basic text for content.</p>
  <a href="#" class="close">Close Fancybox</a>
</div>
```

We also need to slightly change the link to open Fancybox in the `index.html` file:

```
<a id="show-fancybox" href="#">Show The HTML</a>
```

Lastly, we need to change our open function for Fancybox inside the `scripts.js` file:

```
$('#show-fancybox').click(function() {
  $.fancybox.open($('#fancybox-content'));
});
```

Now our Fancybox `open` method contains a jQuery object for the content to display. When you open Fancybox it should look like the following screenshot:

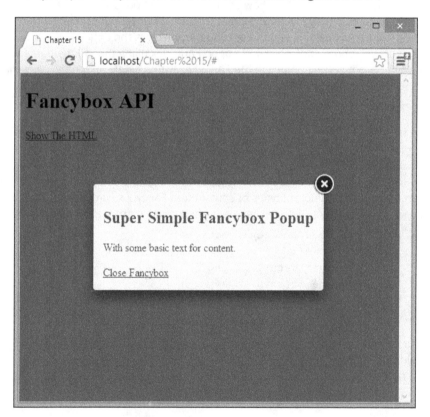

2. Now that we have Fancybox opening our HTML, let's look at using the $.fancybox. close function. This function closes the Fancybox pop up. Let's make the **Close Fancybox** link we have inside the Fancybox pop up, close the pop up.

```
$('.close').on('click', function() {
  $.fancybox.close();
});
```

3. Fancybox has other functions that are advantageous when you have dynamically changing content inside the Fancybox pop up. If you want to tell Fancybox to reposition the location of the pop up, it can be done with a call to the $.fancybox. reposition() function. Fancybox will move the pop up to the appropriate location inside the window.

4. Fancybox also provides us with a function to resize the Fancybox window as required. The $.fancybox.update() function tells Fancybox to resize the height of the Fancybox pop up to match the content. It is necessary when you are programmatically changing the content inside the Fancybox pop up.

5. The $.fancybox.toggle() function will put Fancybox into fullscreen mode, if necessary. It will only have an effect if the content is larger than the current Fancybox pop-up window.

6. You can show and hide the Fancybox loader using the $.fancybox.showLoading() and $.fancybox.hideLoading() functions. These functions are useful when you are processing data inside the Fancybox pop up and want to tell the user that your content or information is loading.

7. The last major function available to us is the $.fancybox.cancel() function. This function will stop loading the Fancybox pop up. It may be useful when the content takes too long to load and you want to just stop (especially if the content is an iframe and the website you are trying to load is not available).

How it works...

The Fancybox API is simply a set of functions that the plugin allows us to call. These functions are exposed to make it easier for us to work with the plugin and have increased control over how the plugin works.

You may have noted that when we created the close link we bound to the click event using the jQuery .on() function. This is because when Fancybox moves the HTML into the Fancybox pop up, the events that have been bound to the objects are reset. By using the .on() function, the event is listened for at the window level (similar to the jQuery .live() function); so no matter where a link with the class of close exists, the event binding will trigger. For more information on event binding and delegation using jQuery, see the jQuery API at http://api.jquery.com/on/.

Manipulating image slideshows (Advanced)

Fancybox also has API methods for interacting with image slideshows. We can use these methods to start or stop playback, move to the next or previous image, and move to any image in the slideshow. Let's create some simple links to move around the slideshow using the API.

Getting ready

We'll start with code similar to that found in the *Creating an image gallery* recipe. The only difference will be that we will include the `styles.css` file so we can add some custom styles.

How to do it...

1. Let's create the HTML and CSS for the custom buttons we are going to have. We'll start with the following HTML code:

```
<div class="custom-controls">
  <a href="#" class="previous">Previous</a>
  <a href="#" class="play-pause">Play</a>
  <a href="#" class="next">Next</a>
  <a href="#" class="random">Random</a>
</div>
```

The HTML we have is a `div` element containing the four links we will use to trigger the API functions.

2. Next let's add some styles to the `styles.css` file to make the `custom-controls` div show all the time:

```
h1 {
   margin-top: 50px;
}

.custom-controls {
   background: white;
   height: 50px;
   line-height: 50px;
   width: 93%;
   position: fixed;
   top: 0px;
   z-index: 9999;
   text-align: center;

}

.custom-controls a {
   padding: 0 15px;
}
```

Note that the links will be visible even when Fancybox is not open. These controls will still work even without Fancybox being displayed. For the sake of brevity, we have not made the controls hide and show with the Fancybox pop up, but I would recommend that you do. With these styles in the `styles.css` file, the `custom-controls` div should look like the following screenshot:

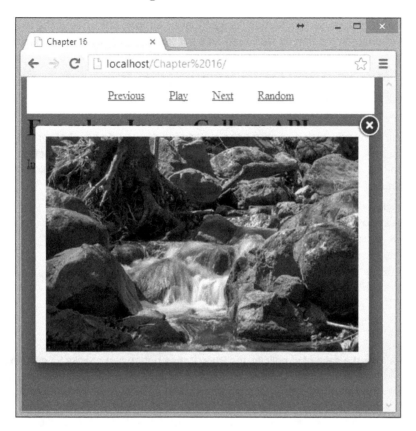

3. Now that we have the HTML and CSS files in place, we can start making our links work. Let's start with the **Previous** link, which will move the slideshow back by one image. First we need to bind to the `click` event. Inside that event binding, we just need to call `$.fancybox.prev()` to move Fancybox to the previous image, as shown in the following code:

```
$('.previous').click(function() {
  $.fancybox.prev();
});
```

4. Next let's make the **Next** link work. This will be exactly the same as the **Previous** link, except we will call `$.fancybox.next()`, as shown in the following code:

```
$('.next').click(function() {
  $.fancybox.next();
});
```

5. The play and pause functionality is also just as simple, but we're going to make the text change on the link as well. First let's set up the functionality, as shown in the following code:

```
$('.play-pause').click(function() {
  $.fancybox.play();
});
```

The link will now play and pause the slideshow, depending on whether or not the slideshow is currently playing. Let's make the button text reflect the action we will be taking, instead of just always saying **Play**. The following code should be used, instead of the previous code:

```
$('.play-pause').click(function() {
  $.fancybox.play();
  if ($(this).text() === 'Play') {
    $(this).text("Pause");
  } else {
    $(this).text("Play");
  }
});
```

 For the sake of simplicity, the **Play/Pause** button just checks its own text to reflect its current state. On a real website, it would be better to listen for the Fancybox events, `onPlayStart` and `onPlayEnd`, and update the text when those are triggered. Events are discussed in the next recipe.

In the previous code, we are still calling the Fancybox API function. We are also checking the text of the `play-pause` link. If the text is `Play` then we set the text to `Pause`. If it is anything other than `Play`, we set it to `Play`. Now our link represents the state of the Fancybox slideshow.

6. The last link is our random link. This link will use the Fancybox API $.fancybox. jumpto method, which moves the slideshow to the image at the provided index. We will be providing a random number between zero and four as the index. First we need to create our random number. JavaScript has a built-in way to get random numbers using the Math.random() function. We will use this to get our random number. We will then provide this random number to the $.fancybox. jumpto() function, as shown in the following code:

```
$('.random').click(function() {
    var randomNumber = Math.floor(Math.random() * 4);

    $.fancybox.jumpto(randomNumber);
});
```

In the previous code, the randomNumber variable is a random integer in the range of zero to three (including three). We provide that to the $.fancybox.jumpto() function and when the **Random** link is clicked on, a random image will display. Note that with this implementation, the image that is being transitioned to may be the same as the one that is currently being displayed.

How it works...

In all of the previous examples, we rely on the jQuery click event binding functionality to bind our click events. All of the bindings are passed an anonymous function, which has our code inside it. However, in the case of the **Next** and **Previous** links, we could simply provide the API function directly without using an anonymous function, as shown in the following code:

```
$('.previous').click($.fancybox.prev);
```

I decided to make all of the click events use anonymous functions to make all of these events consistent to avoid any confusion about differences between the API functions.

The Math.random() function used to generate a random number creates a random number between zero and one. In the previous example, we multiplied it before hand, because we are then left with a number between zero and 3.9999999. Next, we passed this number to the Math.floor function, which rounds the number down to the nearest whole number.

Listening for Fancybox events (Advanced)

Fancybox provides us with a number of different event-driven callback functions that allow us to run code when a certain event occurs. The main callback functions we can use allow us to run code when Fancybox is about to display or hide, when content is about to be loaded or after it is done loading, and when the user plays or pauses the slideshow. We are only going to look at triggering functionality when Fancybox opens and closes and on play/pause. At the end of this recipe is a list of all of the callback functions available in Fancybox.

Getting ready

Let's expand upon the code that we used in the previous recipe. Right now the bar with our links shows all the time regardless of whether or not Fancybox is displaying. Let's make it such that this bar shows and hides when Fancybox is opened and closed. Let's also make Fancybox close when the slideshow is paused.

How to do it...

1. To start with, let's make the bar hidden all the time. We can simply add the `hidden` class to the `custom-controls` div, as shown in the following code:

   ```
   <div class="custom-controls hidden">
   ```

2. Now that the custom controls are hidden on page load, we need to make them display when we open Fancybox. We'll use the `afterShow` callback to make the custom controls show right after Fancybox has finished animating into view. We need to change our call to Fancybox to include this new callback function:

   ```
   $('.fancybox').fancybox({
     afterShow: function() {
       $('.custom-controls').removeClass('hidden');
     }
   });
   ```

   Here we are calling Fancybox with a settings object that only has one setting: `afterShow`. The `afterShow` setting is an anonymous function, in which we remove the `hidden` class from the custom controls.

3. Now our controls show once we open Fancybox, but they continue to show after it is closed. We can use the `beforeClose` callback to run the code to add the `hidden` class back to the `custom-controls` div just as the Fancybox pop up is closing, as shown in the following code:

```
$('.fancybox').fancybox({
    afterShow: function() {
        $('.custom-controls').removeClass('hidden');
    },
    beforeClose: function() {
        $('.custom-controls').addClass('hidden');
    }
});
```

The `custom-controls` div should now hide when Fancybox is closed.

4. Next let's make the Fancybox pop up close when the slideshow is paused. Fancybox has another callback function `onPlayEnd`, which is called when slideshow playback is paused. We'll use this along with the `$.fancybox.close()` API function to make the Fancybox pop up close when the slideshow is paused, as shown in the following code:

```
$('.fancybox').fancybox({
    afterShow: function() {
        $('.custom-controls').removeClass('hidden');
    },
    beforeClose: function() {
        $('.custom-controls').addClass('hidden');
    },
    onPlayEnd: function() {
        $.fancybox.close();
    }
});
```

In the previous code, we are telling Fancybox that the `onPlayEnd` callback should use the anonymous function, which closes the Fancybox pop up. When you play the slideshow nothing should happen, but if you click the link again to pause, the slideshow Fancybox will close.

How it works...

The functions we used here are event driven. This means that behind the scenes, Fancybox is triggering an event when these actions complete and it has an event binding (listens for the event), which then runs the function we provided.

There are more events that we can listen for and are used in the exact same way as the ones we set up in the example. The entire list can be found in the following table, or on the Fancybox website: `http://fancyapps.com/fancybox/#docs`.

Event	Description
onCancel	Called to abort the call to open Fancybox
beforeLoad	Called just before Fancybox starts loading the content it is going to display
afterload	Called just after Fancybox finishes loading the content it is going to display
beforeShow	Called just before Fancybox starts opening
afterShow	Called just after Fancybox finishes opening
beforeClose	Called just before Fancybox starts closing
afterClose	Called just after Fancybox finishes closing
onUpdate	Called after the window is resized to change the orientation of the window (for tablets or phones), or when the user scrolls the window
onPlayStart	Called after the slideshow has started playing
onPlayEnd	Called after the slideshow has been paused

Fancybox is a powerful plugin for jQuery, but it is not the only one. If you want to learn more about other great jQuery plugins, check out `http://plugins.jquery.com/`. If you want to learn how to write your own jQuery plugin, a great starting point is on the jQuery site as well at `http://learn.jquery.com/plugins/`. The jQuery site also has information on events and how to contribute to jQuery, and many other resources at `http://www.jquery.com`.

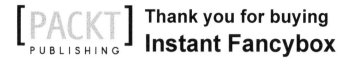
Thank you for buying
Instant Fancybox

About Packt Publishing

Packt, pronounced 'packed', published its first book "*Mastering phpMyAdmin for Effective MySQL Management*" in April 2004 and subsequently continued to specialize in publishing highly focused books on specific technologies and solutions.

Our books and publications share the experiences of your fellow IT professionals in adapting and customizing today's systems, applications, and frameworks. Our solution based books give you the knowledge and power to customize the software and technologies you're using to get the job done. Packt books are more specific and less general than the IT books you have seen in the past. Our unique business model allows us to bring you more focused information, giving you more of what you need to know, and less of what you don't.

Packt is a modern, yet unique publishing company, which focuses on producing quality, cutting-edge books for communities of developers, administrators, and newbies alike. For more information, please visit our website: www.packtpub.com.

Writing for Packt

We welcome all inquiries from people who are interested in authoring. Book proposals should be sent to author@packtpub.com. If your book idea is still at an early stage and you would like to discuss it first before writing a formal book proposal, contact us; one of our commissioning editors will get in touch with you.

We're not just looking for published authors; if you have strong technical skills but no writing experience, our experienced editors can help you develop a writing career, or simply get some additional reward for your expertise.

jQuery UI 1.6: The User Interface Library for jQuery

ISBN: 978-1-84719-512-8   Paperback: 440 pages

Build highly interactive web applications with ready-to-use widgets of the jQuery user interface library

1. Packed with examples and clear explanations to easily design elegant and powerful front-end interfaces for your web applications

2. Organize your interfaces with reusable widgets like accordions, date pickers, dialogs, sliders, tabs, and more

3. Enhance the interactivity of your pages by making elements drag and droppable, sortable, selectable, and resizable

Learning jQuery, Third Edition

ISBN: 978-1-84951-654-9   Paperback: 428 pages

Create better interaction, design, and web development with simple JavaScript techniques

1. An introduction to jQuery that requires minimal programming experience

2. Detailed solutions to specific client-side problems

3. Revised and updated version of this popular jQuery book

Please check **www.PacktPub.com** for information on our titles

jQuery 1.4 Reference Guide

ISBN: 978-1-84951-004-2   Paperback: 336 pages

A comprehensive exploration of the popular JavaScript library

1. Quickly look up features of the jQuery library

2. Step through each function, method, and selector expression in the jQuery library with an easy-to-follow approach

3. Write your own plug-ins using jQuery's powerful plug-in architecture

---

jQuery for Designers: Beginner's Guide

ISBN: 978-1-84951-670-9   Paperback: 332 pages

An approachable introduction to web design in jQuery for non-programmers

1. Enhance the user experience of your site by adding useful jQuery features

2. Learn the basics of adding impressive jQuery effects and animations even if you've never written a line of JavaScript

3. Easy step-by-step approach shows you everything you need to know to get started improving your website with jQuery

Please check **www.PacktPub.com** for information on our titles